Roger M. Scout

"This book reminds us that management is a skill that can be learned and must be continually sharpened. Good functional experts are not automatically good managers, but they can be if they follow Scovil's rules."

—Mark Towery, Managing Director, Fry Consultants

"This book offers a common-sense approach to a very difficult topic to learn and to teach. Reading *Get Ahead* is like having the CEO sit down over coffee with you and tell you the real secrets of management success! These rules are easy to remember and applicable throughout the management chain."

—Lori Clos Fisher, Senior Vice President,
Director of Product Training & Communications,
Global Treasury Services, Bank of America

"Roger Scovil's book *Get Ahead* offers a compact, common-sense approach to management. This easy, thought-provoking read is good for all levels of managers to understand and review."

—Stan Waterhouse, Vice President, Club and Golf,
The Ritz-Carlton Hotel Company, LLC

"A real 'management for dummies.' Worth much more than its weight in gold."

—Jacobus Boers, Director of Marketing,
Excellation Corporation

Get Ahead

SCOVIL'S 7 RULES FOR SUCCESS IN MANAGEMENT

Roger M. Scovil

LONGSTREET PRESS

Atlanta

Published by
LONGSTREET PRESS
2140 Newmarket Parkway
Suite 122
Marietta, GA 30067

Printed in the United States of America

1st printing 2001

Library of Congress Catalog Card Number: 00-111594

ISBN: 1-56352-652-2

Jacket and book design by Burtch Bennett Hunter

⑦ Get Ahead

Dedication

To my daughters:

Frances Scovil, who first asked me to write down
the seven rules for use in her business.

Betty Scovil McKibben, who insisted that I
write a book to go with the rules.

Contents

Preface

One of the most satisfying parts of my forty-six-year business career has been coaching my colleagues and subordinates in working productively in the corporate environment. Although it may seem illogical, I was always gratified when one of my people was promoted to a higher position in another part of the company. On five separate occasions, my protégés were eventually promoted to senior vice president while I was still a vice president.

The first time that happened, I wasn't sure I liked it. But when I thought about it, I realized that what I'd taught him had played a major role in his ascent up the ladder—that, and the fact that he was a lot smarter than I was and richly deserved the promotion.

I then concluded that his promotion honored me. I'd seen this person's potential and trained him to become an excellent manager, and the promotion had confirmed my judgment. I realized that the more often this happened, the more value I could add to my company—and the more I would eventually enhance my own advancement opportunities with my somewhat limited technical brainpower. It worked. After steadily rising through the ranks of my first two companies, I became president of two companies and sat on a number of boards of directors.

One of my former bosses once told me that good managers possess three crucial qualities: they're *smart*, they're *intelligent* and they have the *right philosophy*. By "smart" he meant they have a good memory for facts and figures. By "intelligent" he meant the ability to think logically. And by the "right philosophy" he meant having the proper priorities in life and business. He believed the right philosophy was far more important than the other two.

I can't make you smart. (Anyhow, you've already proven you're smart—you've bought my book.) I can't make you intelligent, either; that depends on your genes, environment, and education. But I can teach you a set of rules that has helped me and many of my colleagues over the years. And these rules can help you develop a philosophy for management success. They aren't hard to apply. But in many cases, they are counter to our natural tendencies. That's why there is such a premium on really good managers. You need to stick this little book in your top drawer after you have read it. Then, refer to the rules a couple of times a week to make sure you are applying them. They work!

A former associate of mine recently called me to tell me he'd been appointed CEO of a major engineering company. Then he thanked me for my help. "I had nothing to do with it," I told him. "Sure you did," he replied. "You helped me develop my management skills—and that's one of the things that got me my new job."

Not long ago, my daughter Frances, a successful manager in her own right, asked me to write down the management rules I'd been talking about all these years so she could use them in her business. When I made the initial list, I came up with six rules. But a few months later a colleague of mine got fired, in spite of my continually pleading with him to either get on his boss's wavelength or go work somewhere else. His failure to do either made the clash inevitable. Shortly after that, another associate made the same mistake—and I realized I had seven rules, not six.

I've stuck to these seven rules because they're basic to management success, because I want to keep this book short and digestible, and because I didn't want to contribute to the information overload that afflicts us all.

I hope this book will make you think about these rules and how often you stray from them. I hope it will improve your management skills and help you add value to your organization. And who knows, it may even make you a nicer person to live with.

RULE 1

Don't Make Enemies

*Sooner or later they will get you.
An enemy may vote to block your
favorite project or a promotion or a
raise you truly deserve . . . or may
even undermine your image
and get you fired.*

I don't know which of my rules is the most important, but I've made this number one, because it is so often the result when you fail to follow one of the other rules. It is also the most common trap into which managers fall.

I'm not saying that it is impossible to be a successful manager if you have enemies. Certainly some of the leaders of major corporations rule with an iron fist, creating enemies both internally and externally. However, you'll have to be a lot smarter to succeed if you have to do it while being surrounded by people who are eager to see you fall on your face.

I have always hoped that I was "smarter than the average bear." But I know there are a lot of people out there who can think and scheme circles around me. I want them on *my* side. Then they will think and scheme to help me *succeed*, rather than thinking and scheming about how to bring me to my knees.

Our company once hired a new business development manager who was very smart, a super salesman, and had plenty of great ideas. He was very good at selling external clients. At first, he was accepted by practically everyone. But he had a failing. He didn't realize he needed to use his selling skills with his *internal* clients as well as his *external* ones. He was one of those people who are always right, at least in their own minds. He was unwilling to compromise with the company's other senior managers. And whenever he couldn't convince them his way was best, he went ahead and did it his way anyhow. Each time he did that, he created another enemy.

After a while, he began to sense the growing opposition within the company. He became paranoid, deciding that everyone was out to get him. At this point, he might have tried making an all-out effort to win over his enemies through compromise and by going along with their suggestions. Instead, he chose confrontation—and lost any chance to patch things up with his internal clients. In the end, of course, they got him. Those coworkers complained to his boss and he lost his job. He'd insisted on doing everything his way, ignored others' ideas and feelings, and he paid the price.

Of course I've oversimplified a complex, real-life situation. However, I am convinced that the primary problem was failure to observe Rule 1.

Years ago, I was a member of a five-person company operating board. It was our job, among other things, to recommend officer appointments to the CEO and board of directors. I remember a time when we had too many highly qualified prospects for a small number of vice president slots. So we were very picky in our recommendations. Occasionally, it took only one negative comment from a board member to sink someone's candidacy. More often than not, that negative comment originated with an enemy the candidate had made somewhere along the line.

If you want to avoid making enemies, start by assuming people are your friends—and treat them accordingly. Paranoia is a sure-fire enemy-creating emotion. If you assume someone is your enemy and treat her as one, she will usually accommodate you by becoming one. Paranoia is contagious.

What do you do if you've already made an enemy, perhaps inadvertently? You do your level best to win back his friendship. Sit down with the person and say something like: "I have the feeling that something is not right between us. I respect you and want to be your friend. What problem do you have with me and how can I correct it to win back your friendship and support?" I have used this approach numerous times throughout my career and it has never failed to improve the atmosphere, often dramatically.

I used this approach with one of my first bosses. I was working for a small construction company during the summers while in engineering school. I was a drafts-man doing piping details for the first launch pad at Patrick Air Force Base, now Kennedy. (The drafting was with pencil and paper, and the calculations were done on a slide rule. I guess that really dates me!)

I was working for a vice president who was only thirty-six, but seemed very old to me. Nothing I did for him was right. Every time he looked at my work he told me—loudly—how screwed up it was. When I did it over, he'd come by and again tell me how wrong it was. I could not please him. I was hurt. My instinctive reaction was anger. I was tempted to go to the big boss and complain.

Instead, I followed some advice my mother had given me years before. I went to him and said "Bill, you seem to be dissatisfied with me. I am doing the best I can with the information and background I have, but you always let me know how stupid I am. What can I do to please you?"

To my amazement, he was completely surprised. He said, "No, you are doing a fine job." I replied, "But you have never said that to me." He then broke down, saying, "Roger, I'm sorry. I have just been promoted to vice president and, not being a college graduate, I feel overwhelmed by the responsibilities of this job. I'm afraid I have been taking it out on you." His behavior toward me changed dramatically after that. He got off my back. He helped me to understand my tasks. I was able to please him. He even complimented me on my work. I'd converted a potential enemy into a good friend.

When my mother advised me not to make enemies, she wasn't thinking about my management skills. She was thinking about life. And I think this rule applies to all of our relationships, not just those we have in business.

Unfortunately, it's easy to make enemies—without meaning to—because of our automatic reactions to various events. I learned that a number of years ago at a weekend workshop called "The Life Training." This course helped me see how a person's automatic reactions can antagonize others, creating enemies that eventually weaken our ability to manage well. I was so impressed with the course that I sent thirty-two of my employees to take it as well. It had a major impact on the way we related to each other in the office. And it helped me turn a money-loser into a winner.

I recommend this short, inexpensive course to anyone, but especially to those who find that they have associates who rub them the wrong way. It changed my management style and helped create much of the philosophy that is in this book. Check the website at http://www.lifetraining.org/ for worldwide times and places.

The nice thing about not having enemies is that it makes work so much more pleasant. We can't often choose to work with our friends, but we can choose to be friends with our coworkers.

Before you go to the next rule, think of the situations in your own company where making an enemy has cost you or an associate in some significant way. Then think of how you can prevent that from happening in the future. The best way is by adopting a positive attitude toward your colleagues and associates, and working diligently to maintain friendly relations with them.

RULE 2

Hire People Who Are
Smarter Than You

They will make you look good.
They will do your work for you.
Smart people hire smarter people.

This rule runs contrary to another basic human instinct. Subconsciously, we tend to think, "If my subordinate is smarter than I am, how can I control her? She will realize that I am not so smart and will undermine me." But unless you disobey some of the other rules, it doesn't work that way.

Most people want to make their bosses look good so they will be rewarded for the success of their part of the enterprise. Of course, they want to be appreciated for doing that because they know that job security and advancement come from recognition of ability and effort.

Early in my career I was given the responsibility to manage a newly formed division of my company. One of the first new people I interviewed was a bright, energetic young man who had just completed the company's training program. I asked him, "What is your goal in the company?" He replied, "To be president." I laughed, "Well, that's ambitious, and maybe you'll make it someday. But what is your shorter range goal?" To my surprise, he said, "I want to get *your* job."

I thought that my hearing had gone bad or that I was finally losing it. Then he elaborated, "I mean, I am going to make you look so good that you will be promoted and I will get your job."

During the next three years he worked enthusiastically to make our division prosper. Soon he was doing most of the work. The division became the most profitable one in the company. After a while, the company established another major new division and I was promoted to vice president and asked to take charge. My former trainee was given my job as division manager.

Incidentally, a few years later he became a senior vice president before I did. I often wonder where I would have been today had I been so insecure as to worry about his taking my job. I would probably still have been back where I started and my protégé would have left the company long ago seeking more responsibility.

Managers are not generally selected for their technical expertise, although a general knowledge of the technical aspects of the business may be important. No, managers are hired to manage the efforts of other people. Many technical experts are failures at managing people. They find it difficult to trust less technically competent subordinates to do difficult jobs.

Not long ago I gave a speech about international business to a group of young entrepreneurs. At the break, the president of a small but highly successful manufacturing company came to me and said, "You are an engineer and come from an engineering company. Where can I find a good engineering manager? I've been searching for one for a year without success." "A good engineering manager?" I replied, with tongue in cheek. "That's an oxymoron." Then I added, "Of course, there are good technical managers, but they are rare. Most people who go into engineering do so because they are fascinated with the technical details. They are not much interested in learning management skills. And many won't hire people who are smarter than they are."

The point is, technical people find it harder than most to hire people who are smarter than they are. And even if they hire them, they often do not manage them in a way that uses their technical skills to their best advantage.

Several years ago, a company that hadn't made profit in ten years hired me as president. My job: to turn it around. One of the problems I had to overcome involved the engineering vice president, a highly respected Ph.D., generally acknowledged to be one of the world's half-dozen top experts in his field. He also had the reputation of being a disaster as a manager.

He was a brilliant, warm, wonderful guy who worked around the clock, but his department was in chaos. A few weeks after my arrival, I went to his office about seven o'clock one evening and found him at his desk working away amid a pile of technical documents.

"What are you working on?" I asked. "I'm trying to solve a difficult technical problem," he replied. I said, "Well, you are one of the top technical experts in the world and you may want to continue that. But, if you are going to manage your department, you'll have to concentrate on management and leave the technical details to the smart people you've hired to do that job. If you want to be a manager, I will work with you to improve your management skills. But you have to choose. Think about it for a couple of days and let me know what you want to do."

When I came into work the next morning, he was waiting to see me. He said, "I've thought about it and decided I want to become a good manager." Over the next few days, we realigned responsibilities in his department so that some of the key, smart subordinates would take over most of the detailed technical work. Over the next two years, we continued to work closely together to improve his management skills. Gradually his reputation changed and he was eventually recognized as being one of the company's better managers.

Two years later, he was offered the job of corporate director of research and development with the parent company in Germany. I hated to lose him, but I was pleased that his management skills had improved so much during our time together that he'd earned such a substantial promotion. It certainly improved my own image in the company as a manager who increased the skills of his people.

Think of examples in your own experience when managers have surrounded themselves with incompetent people who have doomed the enterprise to mediocrity or failure. Successful leaders tend to hire sharp, aggressive people who make them look good and who do their work for them. Do you look for people who are smarter than you to bring into your organization? How many people do you have whom you consider to be smarter than you? If the answer is "none," you probably need to look at your management philosophy and your promotability.

RULE 3

Delegate and Follow Up

Tell your subordinates what needs to be done. Then get out of their way and let them do it.
Let them fail in noncritical tasks so that they can learn. Accept responsibility for those failures.
Follow up positively to avoid major problems but don't nitpick.
Never make a subordinate (or anybody else) look bad. It's a sign of an insecure manager.

I have seen more bright young managers fail because they ignored this rule than for any other reason. In fact, the Engineering VP I mentioned in Rule 2 had also failed because he didn't obey Rule 3.

I have been fortunate to have had wonderful bosses. One of my first, the owner of the small construction company, embodied the proper application of Rule 3, the delegation rule. I started working for him as a laborer and draftsman on a construction job while I was still in school. When I graduated I became a field engineer and then an estimator with the company.

My boss taught me the basics of estimating. He said, "Imagine how long it would take to do each task based on your field experience and convert the time to money." As I completed each estimate, he would review it and add factors for overhead, profit, and contingency. If he felt that my estimate was low, he would add a healthy contingency. If he felt it was high, he reduced the contingency or profit. On those occasions when he found a major error, he would send me back to rework it. But he never changed my figures. And he never made me "wrong."

Occasionally when we lost a bid because I had priced something too high, or when we took a job too low, he would say, "I should have caught that. I knew better but I wouldn't expect you to have known." He always accepted responsibility for *my* mistakes. As a result, I learned a lot very quickly. I also practically worshipped the man because he was so easy to work for. He always made me feel that he had confidence in me; therefore, I tried very hard not to betray that confidence.

The result was that I soon developed the skills and self-confidence to make a lot of money for the company. It was a win for both of us.

Managers need time for strategic planning and to direct the efforts of their subordinates. They also need time for both internal and external selling to make sure they are satisfying all their clients. You can't do that properly if you are immersed in the details of your department's work, unless it is a very small unit.

How good a delegater are you? Do you have good people to whom to delegate? Do you always take responsibility for their failures? When was the last time you made one of your subordinates (or your spouse) look bad? If you don't have good answers to these questions, take time to consider how you can improve this area of your management technique.

RULE 4

Train Your Understudy

Teach a subordinate your job and let him or her do as much of it as he or she can. That will reduce the pressure on you. It will make you available for promotion. Or give you time to work on innovative strategic improvements. And it will make you look smart for picking good people.

This rule is closely related to the two that preceded it, "Hire people who are smarter than you" and "Delegate and follow up." But while those two apply generally to all of your people, Rule 4 is specifically aimed at the relationship between you and your potential successor or successors.

Of course it isn't easy to find an understudy capable enough to learn your job and patient enough to wait for you to be promoted, retire, or leave the company. It is particularly difficult if you have a small staff. But it is vitally important to your company—and even to you.

In the example I gave in Rule 2, the reason I was promoted to vice president was that I had trained my understudy well. I trained him by letting him do more and more of my work. The division I was running was a very important one to the company. Had I not had a well-prepared understudy, I could not have been spared to run the new operation, which included the new title.

My experience in recruiting from within the company is that often people qualified for key promotions can't be moved up because there is no one to take their place.

One of the companies I worked for started as a small, one-man show and became one of the world's largest in its field. As it began to grow, the founder asked a management consulting firm what he should do to prepare the company for continuing growth. The consultants recommended—strongly—that he select and start grooming his understudy. To his credit, the founder followed that advice and named one of his key people president. The new president was young, smart, and ambitious. But he had a lot to learn.

Fortunately, he learned well. The founder died less than ten years later. In the meantime, the company had gone public. By then, the president was well recognized as a capable leader and he had been running most of the operations for several years. The company's market valuation was affected very little by the loss of the founder because of the confidence the investors had in the company's continued management.

In one of our early overseas ventures, we bought controlling interest in a company in our industry in an emerging market country. The company had an excellent reputation for integrity and technical capability. But management problems had prevented it from making much money. It was a mid-sized company in its market, but it was a one-man show.

The general manager was very good at running things, as long as the company was small enough for him to be involved in every project. But the company had grown too large for that. We implemented several management improvements. One of the most important was to insist on the application of Rule 4. Fortunately, there was an excellent young manager on the staff who was an ideal understudy.

To the credit of the general manager, he worked diligently at training his new understudy. Within five years, the general manager left the company to pursue other interests. But the new manager stepped in so that the company continued to function with minimal disruption.

Paranoid managers tend to surround themselves with weak people. They consciously or subconsciously neglect or refuse to train understudies. They are afraid that a smart subordinate will take their job. This is a self-defeating strategy. A manager without an understudy is often a workaholic "superman" or "superwoman" who tries very hard to impress the world with his or her value to the organization. A few people may be fooled, but most recognize such people as possibly valuable technicians, but poor managers.

If you want to create the image of yourself as a good manager, hire an understudy and train him or her to do your job. Set yourself up for promotion and protect your organization from disaster in case of your departure.

Violation of this rule is not limited to inexperienced young managers. Roberto Goizueta, a former CEO of Coca-Cola, was one of the most successful managers of our time. He carefully groomed his understudy, Doug Ivester, for many years. When Goizueta died after a brief illness, Ivester appeared to be well qualified to step into the leadership role of his predecessor. After two years, however, he was pressured by the board to step down. Of course, there were a number of factors that led to this decision. But an important one, as reported by the media, was that the board had asked him to set up a succession plan, which after two years, he hadn't done. They took this as one of the early signs that he lacked some of the critical management skills necessary for this high-profile job. His successor, Doug Daft, appointed his own understudy within two months and the stock price bounded up, partly in appreciation of this strong move.

How many of the managers in your organization have subordinates capable of taking over in case they leave? If they have been in place for a year or more without training an understudy, have they reached their "level of incompetence"? If you had an opportunity for advancement, could you take it or are you too "essential" in your current position? What can you do about it?

RULE 5

Treat All of Your Clients with Respect

Your external clients (that's obvious);
Your internal clients (not so obvious): boss, peers,
associates, subordinates, subcontractors, the janitor;
Your personal clients (even less obvious): spouse,
kids, parents, friends, acquaintances,
neighbors, waitresses, clerks.
If you talk to them with less respect, or act less respectfully
than you do with your best external client, you lose their
respect ... and you may make enemies. (See Rule 1.)
Strong managers get good results without intimidating
people or treating them with contempt.

One of the most confusing things about belonging to an organization is figuring out who your "clients" are. Once you know that, you know whom you must treat with respect. At first thought, it may seem easy. They're the people you're trying to get to buy your products, right? Wrong! Certainly those are *some* of your clients. But your clients also include your associates, boss, subordinates, subcontractors, janitor, spouse, family, friends—virtually anyone from whom you need something or who can directly or indirectly affect your reputation.

In our country, we instinctively know how we must treat our external clients to get and keep their business. It is part of our culture. Treat your customers with respect. What we often don't understand is that there are many others out there who don't buy directly from us, but are equally important to our long-term success. If we don't have their support, we invite failure.

One of my daughters recently went to work for a highly successful major corporation. She had been working for a government agency most of her career. After her first week, she said she had met some of the top executives. "They are the *nicest* people," she said, in surprise. What she hadn't realized was that one of the secrets of success in today's world is to treat others with respect. There are, of course, always a few exceptions. But as I have met the captains of industry and commerce over the years, I have found that most of them are courteous, friendly people. That's part of the reason they got to the top.

The days are long gone when a boss could rant and rave at his subordinates. People today are too mobile. The good ones will go to work somewhere else. In our litigious society, there is also no need to invite lawsuits by making enemies of our employees. We now know that positive reinforcement is a much more effective motivator than negative criticism. We all want to work with other people who are courteous and supportive.

Having said all that, I am continually amazed at the number of people, especially in the lower ranks of employees and new managers, who treat their external clients like kings and some of their associates like trash. That's a great way to remain in the lower ranks, if one remains at all.

I was brought into one company to attempt a turn-around. The CEO of the parent company was worried about the subsidiary's continuing failure to operate profitably. To find out why, he sent one of his trusted people to spend several months with the subsidiary, gather information, analyze the problem, and make recommendations.

The president of the subsidiary and several of his officers knew they were in trouble and they knew the visitor was a "spy." They treated him with the same courtesy we would have given to a Soviet spy at the height of the Cold War. They put him in a room by himself, gave him the absolute minimum information possible, and had as little to do with him as they could. That's called the "mushroom" technique:

"Keep 'em in the dark and feed 'em a lot of $@*#?!" Hardly the way you would treat someone you thought of as a client.

Of course the visitor reported back to the CEO that there were major management problems, that the president should be fired, and that none of the existing executives was capable of replacing him. The president was subsequently dismissed. That's where I came in. When I arrived, I discovered I was surrounded by some very highly qualified executives. They were technical experts. Two of the top three had Ph.D.'s, but their philosophy of management was seriously flawed.

After about a month, while the CEO's representative was still in the office, I went with the business development VP to visit his best client. On the trip to the client's office I said to him, "I am impressed with your background and ability. I think you have the potential to eventually be president of this company. But we need to work on some aspects of your management approach if you are to be considered in the future." He said, "Sure! What do I have to do?"

I continued, "To start, you need to change your approach to one of your clients." "Which client?" he said. "The visitor sent by the CEO to our office," I responded. "Client!" he sputtered. "He's nothing but a damned spy." "Of course he's a spy," I said. "That's why you need to treat him with respect. Everything you say to him goes straight back to the CEO." "Well, I guess you're right. But I'm not going to bow down to him." (Actually he used another verb, but this is a family text.) "Look," I said, "we're going to call on your best external client. I've watched you bow and scrape before that fellow shamelessly." "That's different," he said, "That's sales." "Wait," I countered. "Think about what you just said. Why would you treat an internal client any differently from an external client, especially one who can probably do you more good or harm in the long run than your best external client?" He was silent for a few minutes. Then he said, "Hmm! I see what you mean. I'll give it a try."

To his credit, he completely changed his attitude toward our visitor. Soon I would spot them in the hallway chatting amiably together. At meetings in the home office, this VP would actually seek our friend out and ask him to join him for a meal or a drink. In other words, he started treating him like the "client" that he was. Soon I was getting feedback from headquarters that the VP had greatly improved his management skills. When I left the company a few years later, I was able to recommend him to take over my job. My recommendation was accepted.

Of course this was not the only change he made. But it shows how we were able to change his image by having him treat *all* of his clients with respect.

For several years I've served as the chair of the executive committee of the World Trade Center Atlanta board of directors, as one of my extracurricular activities. Not long ago we contracted with the Ritz-Carlton Management Company to take over the management of our center. This includes operating an elegant dining facility and hosting numerous international meetings and banquets.

I was fortunate enough to be invited to the one-day orientation that the Ritz-Carlton gave the current employees, all of whom remained after the management change. I was greatly impressed with the way the Ritz-Carlton empowered the employees by treating them as they would their best clients.

This approach is embodied in the Ritz-Carlton motto: "We are ladies and gentlemen serving ladies and gentlemen." The company has a number of principles, which they call "basics," one of which is reviewed and discussed each morning with all Ritz-Carlton employees all over the world. For example: "We serve our guests, but we are not servants." The emphasis is on treating external and *internal* clients with the same warm courtesy and respect.

When the facility opened the day after the orientation, it was like a different place. You could feel the staff's renewed enthusiasm, warmth, and pride. Everyone noticed it. In the next few months, revenues doubled. These are the kind of results you can get by making Rule 5 a part of the corporate culture from top to bottom. Treating both your internal and external clients with the same respect is an attribute of good management. Ritz-Carlton's success proves it.

How often have you treated an associate, an acquaintance, the shoe-shine person, or the parking lot attendant differently than you would your best client? If the answer is more often than "never," then there is room for improvement in your management skills, and thereby your chances for promotion. Think of the way other managers in your organization treat people. How do you feel about the management ability of those who don't treat internal clients as well as their external clients? What can you do to improve this aspect of your management skills?

RULE 6

Remember the Organization Chart

Don't give orders to anyone except your direct reports. (See Rule 1.) Communicate with everyone, but keep their respective bosses informed of your contacts— it's a way of showing respect. Work through their bosses and their bosses will reciprocate.

My organization chart rule is really the business version of the "golden rule." Nothing is more disconcerting than having someone come into your business unit and tell your people what to do. Even in loosely structured organizations there are people other than the direct contact who need to know what's going on. When you communicate with someone outside your group, ask yourself: "Who else needs—or would like—to know about this matter? How would I feel if someone came from outside and talked to one of my people like this without informing me?"

An important part of selling is letting your customer know everything he needs to know about your product. In an organization, you are your most important product. If you are going to sell yourself, you must communicate with your internal customers just as you would with an external one. Of course you have to do this discreetly. It can't sound like bragging—or poaching. What you are trying to do is communicate as well as you would to an external client by letting him know what is going on and how he can help you achieve your mutual goals.

This rule also applies when you're talking to people in another organization who may have several contacts within your company. I once called on a customer in my overseas geographical area and learned, to my dismay, that a home office representative had just visited him the week before. This embarrassing turn of events could have easily been avoided had the representative let our local office know he was making contact with our customer. Such thoughtless communication breakdowns do not inspire customer confidence. (Also, see Rule 1.)

A good manager is, by definition, a good communicator. A manager who doesn't communicate well with his or her customers, subordinates, peers, and bosses simply can't manage well. Communication means letting your people know what you are doing, asking them to contribute to the effort, and finding out what they are doing.

It means letting your own team members know what you expect from them and coaching them—without constantly looking over their shoulders—to achieve the results you want. It also means letting other managers and their team members know what you are doing and how they can help you accomplish the corporate goals.

What's the best way to communicate? Many would say E-mail. E-mail is great for informing others of your needs and deeds quickly and efficiently, but it is often responsible for communications overkill—too much of a good thing. And it doesn't carry the information that comes from one's tone of voice.

Remember, when it comes to communication, Murphy's Law applies. If your message *can* be misinterpreted, it *will* be misinterpreted. Thus, E-mail is no substitute for an occasional meeting or a more frequent phone call. Your facial expression or tone of voice can often allow you to disagree without seeming disrespectful.

On one occasion, my company assigned me the management of a consistently unprofitable overseas subsidiary. I soon found one of the problems was that previous management apparently thought it a sign of weakness to let the home office know what was going on or to ask for help—to call on the home office's ample resources to solve problems. After a few months, we had the situation turned around and had become profitable. I was surprised to hear my boss tell the CEO that one reason for the turnaround was that the telephone bill had tripled! That's not what I was accustomed to hearing when overhead went up. My boss, however, realized it was evidence we were communicating better with the home office.

Manager paranoia is another obstacle to good communication. Paranoid managers are easy to spot. They forbid their employees to contact or be contacted by people in certain other parts of the organization. Such people are fairly common, but they rarely reach a company's top echelons. Paranoia is a self-fulfilling emotion that stifles communication and breeds enemies. If you think someone is out to get you, your reactions will create the enemy you fear.

Good teamwork requires good communication between *all* members of the team. Strong managers encourage healthy communication between their team members and other parts of the organization. But good communication does not mean giving orders to someone else's people. Find out what instructions need to be issued by talking to the people involved. Then ask their boss to issue the directive.

How are the communication skills in your organization? Can you think of an occasion when someone disrupted your unit by giving an order to one of your people without your knowledge? How did it make you feel toward that person? Have you ever done it yourself? Do you always have the information you need to run your operation without coming into conflict with other parts of the organization? Do the other managers have good information about your unit? Think about ways you can improve your communication skills.

RULE 7

Get on Your Boss's Wavelength

Try to understand what success looks like to your boss. If you think you have a better approach, try to sell him or her on it. If he or she doesn't buy it, then do it his or her way with enthusiasm. If you can't do that, go work for someone else.

This one seems pretty obvious, doesn't it? Yet I have seen some managers rise to great heights only to be destroyed when they failed to practice this simple rule.

A few years ago, I worked with a very capable manager who reported to the CEO of our company. He was a person of great vision. In my opinion, his vision of the company's future direction was clearer in many ways than the CEO's. He tried to convince his boss that we should move in that direction. He failed. However, he was so certain he was right that he decided he would push in that direction anyway. He started initiatives that were counter to the CEO's direction. He and the CEO had heated arguments about it. I counseled him to accept the

79

CEO's position. He could not. So I encouraged him to look for another job. But he was determined to stay there and prove the CEO wrong. The CEO put up with it patiently until one day it became more than he could handle. My associate walked into my office utterly stunned and surprised and told me he'd been fired.

Years ago, when I was working on construction jobs, I learned a saying: "He may be right and he may be wrong, but he's still the boss!" How do people advance to high levels of management and forget that simple fact?

Many of us have found ourselves dealing with uncomfortable organizational changes or new bosses we just don't understand. Usually, we can can adjust to the situation or to the new boss's style and management philosophy. We may even be able to shape his or her thinking or alter the situation more to our liking. But sometimes, we can't adjust to the new reality and we can't adjust the new reality to suit our preferences. The situation may become difficult, even untenable.

Fifty years ago, employees were loyal to the company because the company was loyal to them. It took care of them in good times and bad. Jobs weren't easy to come by, so employees put up with difficult situations or bosses, even when they were unhealthy for the employee, the boss, and the company. Nowadays, we don't have many of those constraints. Downsizing changed the loyalty quotient. A tight labor market has made it easier to move from company to company. And unless you're downright promiscuous about changing jobs, it's no longer a stigma to move up the ladder company by company. Furthermore, managers are no longer prepared to tolerate team members who prefer to call their own signals.

That does not lessen a good manager's obligation to communicate his ideas and needs to his boss. Nor does it lessen the obligation to do your best to see things the boss's way and to enthusiastically pursue her goals. This is particularly crucial in today's more loosely structured corporate environment where the boss isn't always available, or when it isn't even obvious who the boss is. There may even be several. (A hint for the seriously confused: Your boss is almost certainly the same person who conducts your performance appraisals and determines your compensation.)

It may take you a while to realize you simply can't get on your boss's wavelength. I've faced that situation myself. I'd been working, quite happily, under one company president when a new one took his place. At the end of his first year, he called me to his office and gave me a very mediocre review, substantially lower than my previous one. When I asked why, he pointed out several instances of what he considered to be poor performance before he came on board. I showed him that although it wasn't obvious from the bare numbers, my actions had actually saved the company millions of dollars, and my previous boss had given me high praise and superior ratings as a result. "Oh, I didn't know that," said the new president. But he didn't change the rating. I could see we were on different wavelengths.

For the next several months I tried diligently to understand what the young president wanted me to do. But I gradually concluded that we were coming from such different viewpoints that I would probably never be able to satisfy him. I didn't actively look for another job because I was a longtime employee with many incentives not to leave. But I had my antennae up. Within a few months a headhunter called and, for the first time in my tenure with the company, I responded. A few months later, I left for a far more lucrative job with much more responsibility.

Rule 7 isn't intended to convince middle managers to leave their jobs or their companies. On the contrary, it should encourage them to strive to understand their bosses and to enthusiastically execute their bosses' plans and policies. However, I am encouraging those who can't find a way to play on the team to quit before they get fired. That is a win-win solution to a difficult problem. The employee gets away from an untenable situation gracefully, and the company doesn't have to fire him. Involuntary terminations don't help anyone. And they don't look very good on a resume. If you have to leave, don't burn bridges. (See Rule 1.)

Do you know people in your organization who just can't seem to get on the boss's wavelength? How about you? Are you on your boss's wavelength? If not, are you doing your best to get him to understand where you are coming from? Does he accept your ideas? If he does not, can you do it his way—with enthusiasm? Can you change either the boss's attitude or your own, or do you need to look elsewhere?

Conclusion

Being a good manager is one of the most rewarding of occupations. It is rewarding not only financially, but psychologically as well. Managing the efforts of other people to maximize their productivity and effectiveness multiplies the manager's efforts many times over. If a good manager can increase the productivity of a ten-person team by ten percent more than an average manager, she saves the equivalent of one full salary. If she is managing 1,000 people and performs as well, she saves the equivalent of 100 salaries. That goes right to a company's bottom line and it's the kind of good work that impresses higher management.

People who are truly effective at managing the efforts of others are rare. That's why the law of supply and demand continues to push management compensation skyward. And yet the rules of good management are simple. Anyone can follow them, but few do so consistently. That means you have an opportunity. Make yourself a good manager and you'll have the opportunity to become one of the few—and get paid accordingly.

You don't have to be a technical genius, a financial guru, or a super salesman to be a good manager. You have to surround yourself with technical geniuses, financial gurus, and super salesmen, treat them with respect, delegate wisely to them, train them, and get out of their way so that they can do their jobs. You have to put your ego away and help your people surpass you. You have to build and lead your team enthusiastically, carrying out your boss's program while applying the golden rule when you deal with other parts of the organization. If you can do these things consistently as you pursue your career, without making enemies, your chances of success will skyrocket. Go for it!

Scovil's 7 Rules for Success in Management

RULE 1
Don't Make Enemies
Sooner or later they will get you. An enemy may vote to block your favorite project or a promotion or a raise you truly deserve...or may even undermine your image and get you fired.

RULE 2
Hire People Who Are Smarter Than You
They will make you look good. They will do your work for you. Smart people hire smarter people.

RULE 3
Delegate and Follow Up
Tell your subordinates what needs to be done. Then get out of their way and let them do it. Let them fail in noncritical tasks so that they can learn. Accept responsibility for those failures. Follow up positively to avoid major problems but don't nitpick. Never make a subordinate (or anybody else) look bad. It's a sign of an insecure manager.

RULE 4
Train Your Understudy
Teach a subordinate your job and let him or her do as much of it as he or she can. That will reduce the pressure on you. It will make you available for promotion. Or give you time to work on innovative strategic improvements. And it will make you look smart for picking good people.

RULE 5
Treat All of Your Clients with Respect

*Your external clients (that's obvious); Your internal clients
(not so obvious): boss, peers, associates, subordinates, subcontractors, the janitor; Your personal clients (even less obvious):
spouse, kids, parents, friends, acquaintances, neighbors, waitresses, clerks. If you talk to them with less respect, or act less
respectfully than you do with your best external client, you lose
their respect ... and you may make enemies. (See Rule 1.)
Strong managers get good results without intimidating people
or treating them with contempt.*

RULE 6
Remember the Organization Chart

*Don't give orders to anyone except your direct reports. (See
Rule 1.) Communicate with everyone, but keep their respective
bosses informed of your contacts—it's a way of showing respect.
Work through their bosses and their bosses will reciprocate.*

RULE 7
Get on Your Boss's Wavelength

*Try to understand what success looks like to your boss. If you
think you have a better approach, try to sell him or her on it.
If he or she doesn't buy it, then do it his or her way with
enthusiasm. If you can't do that, go work for someone else.*

Acknowledgments

It would fill another book to list the dozens of friends who have read the drafts of this one. They have given me helpful feedback, constructive criticism, and, most of all, insistent enthusiasm for seeing it published. Here are some who have played key roles:

My friend and longtime Atlanta World Trade Center fellow board member Carl Mittelstadt. Carl, senior partner at CRD marketing consultants in Atlanta, really got me off dead center by enthusiastically insisting that I get the book published and putting me in contact with someone who could point me in the right direction for doing so.

Diane Tanger was that someone. Diane, an associate

of Carl at CRD, guided managing partner Max Carey in publishing his recent book, *The Superman Complex*. She knew which buttons to push.

Harvey Ardman, the professional writer who made my amateur writing come alive. He converted my black-and-white drafts to 3-D color.

Galvan Haun, the talented graphic artist who created the original cover and text design that helped me get a publisher's attention.

Scott Bard, publisher and president of Longstreet Press, and his capable staff, who saw enough potential in this first-time author to take the gamble. His staff includes Tysie Whitman, Ann Lovett, and

Burtch Hunter. They guided me through the bewildering maze of publishing and produced the attractive work that is my book.

Lori Clos Fisher, senior vice president of NationsBank, who had the idea of using the "seven rules" for corporate training. She guided me in the preparation of training manuals and tested my program successfully in her company.

And last, but by no means least, my patient wife and helpmate of forty-seven years, MaryEarle Nock Scovil. In addition to being a great "corporate wife," she followed me through twelve years of overseas assignments while I gained the management experience that made this book possible.

Training materials for
GET AHEAD

The following training materials are currently available for corporate or academic instruction:

Student workbook
Instructor's manual
PowerPoint presentation

For availability, prices, and ordering information, please check our website at:

scovils7rules.com

or write us at:

Scovil's Seven Rules
Suite 150
6025 Riverwood Drive
Atlanta, Georgia
30328-3732